P9-BZT-684

ORVILLE REDENBACHER'S POPCORN COOKBOOK

SMITHMARK

INTRODUCTION

Popcorn has a history that extends back centuries. Thousand-year-old popcorn kernels have been found by archaelogists in Inca Indian tombs and both Christopher Columbus and Hernando Cortes observed native Indians making popcorn decorations and corsages when they explored the Americas. Since first being cultivated from native American grasses to one man's 40 year quest to develop the perfect gourmet hybrid, popcorn has proven itself as more than just a fun snack food.

That's right. Not only is popcorn a fun snack, it's also healthy and nutritious. Popcorn is a good source of essential fiber, contains no salt, sugar, artificial additives or preservatives and is low in calories. It's recommended by the American Cancer Society, the American Dietetic Association and the American Dental Association. And, there's no one who knows the health benefits of popcorn better than Orville Redenbacher, fondly known to many as America's Popcorn King.

Today, his name is a household word and synonymous with high quality, while his Orville Redenbacher's®Gourmet® Popping Corn is the number one selling brand in the country. Born in 1907 and raised in Indiana, Orville's taste for popcorn was homegrown . . . in the family garden. He earned some of his first spending money by selling the popcorn he grew on the the family farm. Orville began his quest for the perfect kernel in earnest in the 1920s when he got involved with popcorn hybridization at Purdue University. He then devoted more than 40 years to research and cross-bred over 30,000 popcorn hybrids to cultivate a kernel that popped up light and fluffy every time.

Determined to market his Gourmet® Popping Corn on high quality rather than low price, Orville literally trekked across the country in 1971 to convince store owners that his popcorn was better tasting than other brands. He then teamed up with Hunt-Wesson, Inc. and in just a few short years, his Gourmet® Popping Corn became the country's number one selling brand.

Orville Redenbacher's® remains the top popcorn today because of Orville's high standards for quality. It is this commitment to perfection that makes Orville Redenbacher's® different from the competition. Grown only by farmers with especially fertile fields, the popcorn is carefully harvested and conditioned to ensure maximum popping performance. The special care and treatment that goes into Orville Redenbacher's Gourmet® Popping Corn helps make it the lightest and fluffiest available.

And, Gary Redenbacher, Orville's grandson shares his grandfather's commitment to high-quality, great-tasting Gourmet® Popping Corn. Today, Gary carries on the Redenbacher family tradition of quality so that future generations of popcorn lovers can enjoy this great tasting popping corn.

In fact, past generations enjoyed the taste of popcorn as well. Popcorn even put in a guest appearance at the first Thanksgiving. Quadequina, brother of the Wampanoag Indian chieftain Massosoit, brought a big deerskin bag of popcorn to the celebration as an offering of friendship. But the Indians held some superstitions about popcorn and what made it pop. Many believed that inside each kernel lived a demon who got angry when put near the heat and it exploded!

Today, the superstitions have been put aside – we know that when the moisture inside each kernel is heated and turns to steam, popcorn pops! And pop it does since every man, woman and child in the United States eats at least 52 quarts per year. It's clear that popcorn is extremely "pop"ular today. And thanks to Orville Redenbacher's®, popcorn lovers everywhere can continue to enjoy the lightest and fluffiest popcorn imaginable.

CLB 2597
©1992 Colour Library Books Ltd, Godalming, Surrey, England.
© Recipes Hunt-Wesson Inc.
All rights reserved.
This edition published 1992 by
SMITHMARK Publishers Inc., 112 Madison Avenue, New York, NY 10016.
Printed and bound in Singapore.
ISBN 0 8317 3192 3

SMITHMARK books are available for bulk sales promotion and premium use. For
details write or telephone the Manager of Special Sales, SMITHMARK Publishers Inc.,
112 Madison Avenue, New York, NY 10016. (212) 532-6600

ORVILLE REDENBACHER IS A REGISTERED TRADEMARK OF HUNT-WESSON INC.

TRIATHLON TURTLES
Makes 30 turtles

You'll never see a turtle move more quickly than when tri-flavored treats are let loose!

1½ quarts popped Orville Redenbacher's Gourmet Original Popping Corn, unsalted, unpopped kernels discarded
1 (14oz) bag light caramels, unwrapped
2 Tbsps *each*: butter or margarine and milk
30 pecan halves
30 whole cashews
1 (6oz) pkg. semi-sweet chocolate morsels
1 tsp shortening

---

1. Have ready a baking sheet lined with lightly greased wax paper.

2. In large bowl, place popped corn; set aside.

3. In medium saucepan, over low heat, combine caramels, butter and milk; stir until smooth.

4. Pour over popped corn, tossing gently to coat.

5. With lightly-greased hands,* press together a Tablespoonful of caramel-coated corn; place onto baking sheet.

6. Using thumb, make a small indentation on top of *each* mound.

7. While popcorn mounds are still warm, place small end of the cashew into the popcorn mound to form the "head". Repeat using *remaining* cashews.

STEP 7

8. In small saucepan, stir together chocolate and shortening until blended.

9. Spoon *1 teaspoonful* of chocolate mixture into indentation for *each* turtle.

10. Place *1 pecan* half into *each* chocolate mound for "shell". Chill until chocolate hardens.

STEP 5

STEP 10

Cook's Notes

🕐 TIME: Preparation and cooking takes about 40 minutes.

🍴 COOK'S TIP:* Use caution when handling popcorn mixture; it may be hot.

❓ VARIATION: Tin-O-Turtles! Present turtles in fancy tins for an extra special gift from your kitchen. Don't forget to place the turtles in candy wrappers to avoid sticking together.

NINA'S TOFFEE FUDGE SQUARES

Makes 4 dozen squares

Nina, Orville's wife, makes triple batches of this fudge for her friends during the holidays. You haven't had fudge, until you've tried Nina's!

Wesson No-Stick Cooking Spray
1 bag popped Orville Redenbacher's Gourmet
    Butter Toffee Microwave Popping Corn,
    unpopped kernels discarded and lightly
    crushed
½ lb (2 sticks) butter or margarine
3 cups semi-sweet chocolate morsels
3¾ cups sugar
1 (12oz) can evaporated milk
½ tsp salt
1½ cups chopped nuts
1 Tbsp vanilla

STEP 5

speed, then high speed for 10 minutes, scraping sides of bowl as needed.

6. Add nuts and vanilla; stir to blend.

7. Carefully spread fudge over popcorn. Top with *remaining* popcorn.

1. Have ready a 13 x 9 x 2-inch baking dish sprayed with cooking spray.

2. Evenly spread 2 cups crushed popcorn in the pan; set aside. Reserve remaining popcorn for topping.

3. In large bowl, place butter and chocolate; set aside.

4. In large saucepan, combine sugar, evaporated milk and salt; bring to boil over low heat, stirring constantly. Then boil on medium heat, stirring constantly, for 14 minutes.

5. Pour over butter and chocolate; blend on low

STEP 7

8. Chill 2 hours or until firm. Cut in 1½-inch squares.

Cook's Notes

⏱ TIME: Preparation and cooking takes 35 minutes.

❓ VARIATION: Nuts to you! Almonds complement and taste exceptionally good in this recipe. Nina likes coarsely chopped and always lightly toasted slivered almonds. Or, if pecans or macadamias are your favorite nut . . . try it, you'll like it!

KISSING IN THE CLOUDS

Makes 16 cookies

These candy-kissed cookies will find their way to anyone's heart!

2 egg whites at room temperature
⅛ tsp salt
¾ cup sugar
½ tsp almond extract
1½ cups flaked coconut
2 cups popped Orville Redenbacher's Gourmet Original Popping Corn, finely crushed*
1 Tbsp all-purpose flour
1 tsp unsweetened dry cherry-flavored drink mix (optional)
16 chocolate candy kisses, unwrapped

1. Preheat oven to 300°F. Have ready a lightly greased baking sheet.

2. In medium bowl, with electric mixer, beat egg whites and salt until frothy.

3. Gradually add sugar, beating continuously until firm peaks form. (Takes about 7 minutes.)

STEP 3

STEP 4

4. By hand, fold in *remaining* ingredients *except* chocolate candy, just until *all* ingredients are moistened.

5. Drop by rounded Tablespoons, two inches apart, on baking sheet.

6. Bake for 1 minute or until set.

7. Remove from oven and immediately gently press a chocolate kiss in center of *each* cookie.

STEP 7

8. Return to oven and bake an additional 8 minutes or until light golden brown; cool 1 minute.

Cook's Notes

⏱ TIME: Preparation and cooking takes 40 minutes.

◣ PREPARATION: *To finely crush popcorn, use a blender or food processor.

🍳 COOK'S TIP: Whip Tip! Down on the farm in Indiana, Orville's grandson, Gary, would collect fresh eggs from the hen house for this recipe. They were always at room temperature – be sure yours are too! They'll whip up perfectly!

OATY-APRICOT GEMS

Makes 28 cookies

These hi-fiber cookies will be a treasured recipe for years to come.

¾ cup firmly packed light brown sugar
¾ cup vegetable shortening
1 egg, lightly beaten
2 Tbsps milk
1½ cups quick-cooking oats
¾ cup all-purpose flour
1 tsp cinnamon
½ tsp *each*: baking powder, baking soda and
    allspice
3 cups popped Orville Redenbacher's Gourmet
    Original Popping Corn, unpopped kernels
    discarded
1 cup chopped dried apricots
½ cup finely chopped walnuts

---

1. Preheat oven to 350°F. Have ready two lightly greased baking sheets.

2. In bowl, combine first 4 ingredients.

3. In another bowl, combine oats, flour, cinnamon, baking powder, baking soda and allspice. Add to sugar mixture; blend well.

4. Add *remaining* ingredients; mix thoroughly.

STEP 4

5. Drop by rounded Tablespoonfuls onto baking sheet.

STEP 3

STEP 5

6. Bake for 12 minutes or until lightly browned.

Cook's Notes

🕐 TIME: Preparation and baking takes 30 minutes.

❓ VARIATION: Nifty Nina. Nina, Orville's wife, will substitute 1 cup chopped dried apples for the apricots when she feels like a change.

SICILIAN OLIVE TREE MEATBALLS

Makes 6½ dozen

These meatballs, with their surprise centers, are delightfully delicious.

Wesson No-Stick Cooking Spray
2 lbs lean ground beef
2 cups Orville Redenbacher's Gourmet Original
   Popping Corn, unpopped kernels discarded
   and finely crushed*
¼ cup chopped parsley
2 Tbsps *each*: grated Parmesan cheese and instant
   onion
1 Tbsp Worcestershire sauce
½ tsp *each*: garlic powder and pepper
2 eggs
1 (10oz) jar stuffed, small, green olives, drained

Sauce
1 (27oz) can Hunt's Homestyle Spaghetti Sauce
2 Tbsps grated Parmesan cheese
2 Tbsps Marsala wine

STEP 3

4. Place on baking sheet and bake 20 minutes.

STEP 4

1. Preheat oven to 350°F. Have ready a baking sheet coated with cooking spray.

2. In mixing bowl, combine beef, popcorn, parsley, Parmesan cheese, onion, Worcestershire sauce, garlic powder, pepper and eggs; mix well.

3. Using a mounded half-Tablespoon, form meat mixture into balls, placing *one olive* in the center of *each* ball, covering completely.

5. Meanwhile, in saucepan, combine *all* sauce ingredients; simmer for 10 minutes. When meatballs are done, add to sauce. Serve hot with toothpicks.

Cook's Notes

TIME: Preparation takes 45 minutes, baking takes 20 minutes.

VARIATION: Lotsa Pasta! Mound meatballs and sauce over strings and strings of hot cooked pasta – it's a wonderful main course for a crowd.

PREPARATION: *To finely crush popcorn, use a blender or food processor.

COOK'S TIP: Meatballs can be made ahead of time and frozen. Bake as directed, cool, bag, then freeze.

GARY'S STUFFED MUSHROOMS

Makes 18-24 stuffed mushrooms

Orville's grandson, Gary, introduced us to these garlic, cheese and popcorn appetizers . . . good going, Gary!

2 Tbsps butter or margarine

1 lb medium to large mushrooms, washed, stems chopped

1½ Tbsps chopped fresh parsley

2 tsps crushed fresh garlic

¼ tsp basil

2½ cups popped Orville Redenbacher's Gourmet Original Popping Corn, unpopped kernels discarded and finely crushed*

¾ cup grated Parmesan cheese

1. Preheat oven to 350°F.

2. In medium non-stick skillet, sauté in butter, mushroom stems, parsley, garlic and basil for 2 to 3 minutes.

STEP 2

STEP 3

3. Remove from heat; stir in popcorn and Parmesan until moistened.

STEP 4

4. Fill mushroom caps with stuffing mixture.

5. Place stuffed mushrooms, filled side up, on baking sheet. Bake for 10 to 15 minutes or until heated through.

Cook's Notes

⏲ TIME: Preparation and cooking takes 30 minutes.

◣ PREPARATION:* To finely crush popcorn, use a blender or food processor.

❓ VARIATION: Nina's Stuffed Mushrooms. Make these stuffed mushrooms the way Gary's Grandmother, Nina, does . . . with ¼ cup cooked sausage. Look out though, they'll be gone before you know it.

CORNY CHIHUAHUA CHEESE SPREAD
Makes 1 corn shaped cheese spread

And we mean corny, 'cause it taste like corn and looks like corn, too. Chihuahua is for the South-of-the-Border taste!

5½ cups popped Orville Redenbacher's Gourmet Butter Microwave Popping Corn, unpopped kernels discarded
1 (8oz) pkg. cream cheese, softened
¼ cup *each*: chopped walnuts and Rosarita Mild Chunky Picante Sauce
1 Tbsp fresh, chopped cilantro
1 tsp chili powder
¼ tsp *each*: ground cumin and garlic powder
1 small head romaine lettuce, separate leaves and reserve core
Crackers

1. Set aside *3 cups* popped corn; finely crush *remaining* popcorn.

2. In medium bowl, blend *crushed* popcorn and *remaining* ingredients *except* reserved popcorn, romaine lettuce, core and crackers. Refrigerate for 20 minutes until cream cheese mixture is slightly firm.

3. Place cheese mixture on serving platter. Lightly butter fingers and shape mixture to form an ear of corn.

STEP 3

4. Place the lighter-colored and smaller-sized leaves and core at the base of the cheese "ear" to look like corn husks. Chill at least 20 minutes.

5. Just before serving, lightly press *remaining* popped corn into cheese mixture to completely cover the "ear". Serve with crackers.

STEP 5

Cook's Notes

TIME: Preparation takes about 35 minutes.

PREPARATION: To finely crush poporn, use a blender or food processor.

SERVING IDEA: You're-A-Star! Impress your family and friends when you prepare this easy, picture-perfect appetizer for your Thanksgiving buffet.

CRISPY CRUNCHY ONION RINGS

Makes 2 servings

Next to popcorn, Orville loves onion rings. Here, he shares his secret recipe.

Wesson Oil
1 extra-large onion
2½ cups popped Orville Redenbacher's Gourmet Original Popping Corn, finely crushed *
¾ cup all-purpose flour
½ tsp baking powder
Salt to taste
¼ tsp *each*: garlic powder and paprika
1 cup buttermilk

1. In 4-quart saucepan, heat 1½ inches oil to 350°F.

2. Cut onion into thick slices then separate into rings; set aside.

STEP 2

3. In a medium bowl, mix *remaining* ingredients *except* buttermilk.

4. Dip onions, one at a time, in flour mixture, then into buttermilk and finally coat well in flour mixture again.

STEP 4

5. Fry onions 3 or 4 at a time until golden brown.

STEP 5

Cook's Notes

🕐 TIME: Preparation and cooking takes 30 minutes.

◣ PREPARATION:* To finely crush popcorn, use a blender or food processor.

❓ VARIATION: Dredge-A-Veg. Try substituting sliced zucchini, sweet potatoes, carrots or just about any vegetable imaginable for the onions in this recipe.

FULL MOON HARVEST BLEND

Makes 1½ quarts

When the summer has turned Indian, it's time to fix yourself a warm batch of this mix.

---

1 (2oz) bag popped Orville Redenbacher's
    Gourmet Caramel Microwave Popping Corn,
    unpopped kernels discarded
1 cup *each*: dried apples, cut into ½-inch pieces
    and raisins
1½ tsps pumpkin pie spice
½ tsp ground ginger
¼ tsp allspice

---

1. Pop corn according to package directions *except do not* spread coated caramel corn on baking sheet; place in large bowl.

STEP 1

2. Immediately stir in apples and raisins.

STEP 2

3. Combine *remaining* ingredients in a small bowl and sprinkle over corn and fruit, tossing gently to coat.

STEP 3

Cook's Notes

⏱ TIME: Preparation takes 15 minutes.

🍞 COOK'S TIP: Warm and Cozy! These taste great warm. Place popcorn mixture in a 200°F oven for 10 minutes. Serve immediately.

HONEY NUT CORN CRUNCH

Makes 10 cups

Make a beeline to the kitchen and whip up a batch of this snack mix!

2 qts. popped Orville Redenbacher's Gourmet Original Popping Corn, unpopped kernals discarded
1 (5oz) can LaChoy Chow Mein Noodles
5 Tbsps butter or margarine
3 Tbsps sugar
3 Tbsps honey
2 tsps vanilla extract
½ tsp ground cinnamon
1 (10oz) can honey roasted peanut cashew mix
½ cup raisins

1. Preheat oven to 250°F. Have ready a lightly greased baking sheet.

2. In a medium mixing bowl, combine popcorn and noodles; set aside.

3. In a small saucepan, melt butter, sugar and honey; stir in vanilla and cinnamon.

STEP 3

4. Pour butter mixture over popcorn mixture; toss until well coated.

STEP 4

5. Spread coated popcorn onto baking sheet. Bake for 1 hour, stirring 3 times during baking; cool.

STEP 5

6. Pour baked popcorn mixture in serving bowl, add peanut mix and raisins; mix well.

Cook's Notes

⏱ TIME: Preparation takes 10 minutes, baking takes 1 hour.

📖 COOK'S TIP: Pardon Me! You *must* "burp" your zip top bags or plastic containers to make them completely airtight before storing popcorn recipes.

OLD FASHIONED STICK-BALL SNAX

Makes 14 cups

American favorites, popcorn, cheese and pretzels, create the base for this 1-2-3-4 ingredient snack.

1 bag popped Orville Redenbacher's Gourmet
    Cheddar Cheese Microwave Popping Corn,
    unpopped kernels discarded
2 cups pretzel sticks
2 cups cheese puff balls
1 cup raisins

Adding ingredients

Preparing the popcorn

1. In a large serving bowl, stir together popped corn, pretzels, cheese puff balls and raisins; mix well.

Mixing ingredients

Cook's Notes

🕐 TIME: Preparation takes 10 minutes.

🍳 COOK'S TIP: Weighty What Not.
Popcorn is 12% protein, 75% carbohydrate and 4% fat. Remember, too, it is high in fiber and low in calories. What a snack!

MIGHTY MEATY MIX

Makes 3 Quarts

An armchair must while watching any sporting event.

1 bag popped Orville Redenbacher's Gourmet Natural Microwave Popping Corn, unpopped kernels discarded
1 (.82oz) pkg. brown gravy mix

2 Tbsps Orville Redenbacher's Buttery-flavor Popcorn Oil
1 (1.2oz) pkg. beef jerky, snipped in pieces

1. Place popcorn in brown paper bag, sprinkle with gravy mix and shake; pour oil over and shake again. Place in large bowl and stir in beef jerky pieces.

POPCORN AT THE RANCH

Makes 3 Quarts

Saddle up and tighten the reins – this popcorn will gallop its way into your mouth faster than you can say . . . "Whoa!"

3 quarts popped Orville Redenbacher's Gourmet Original Popping Corn, unpopped kernels discarded
1 Tbsp or (0.4oz pkg) dry ranch-style salad dressing mix

½ tsp dry dill weed
¼ cup Wesson Oil

1. Pour popped corn into a large brown paper bag; sprinkle corn with dressing mix and dill weed. Close bag and shake vigorously until popcorn is well blended.

2. Pour oil over seasoned popcorn and shake until well coated.

DON JUAN'S WHAT-A-PARTY MIX

Makes 3 Quarts

Don Juan is famous for many things, and his recipe will surely make your party memorable.

3 quarts popped Orville Redenbacher's Gourmet Original Popping Corn, unpopped kernels discarded
¾ tsp *each*: chili powder and garlic salt

¼ tsp cayenne pepper
2 Tbsps butter or margarine, melted

1. Place popcorn in a large serving bowl; set aside.

2. In a small bowl, blend together chili powder, garlic salt and cayenne pepper. Sprinkle over popcorn and toss until evenly coated. Pour butter over popcorn; stir well.

Cook's Notes

🕐 TIME: The Meaty Mighty Mix takes 10 minutes, Popcorn at the Ranch takes 15 minutes, and the Party Mix takes 15 minutes.

❓ VARIATION: Time Out. You can substitute salami or pepperoni for the beef jerky in the Mighty Meaty Mix.

ORANGE CURRIED PORK CHOPS

Serves 6

We've tripled the flavor of orange, mixed it with curry and topped it over popcorn-coated pork. Mmm . . . !

Wesson No-Stick Cooking Spray
1 quart popped Orville Redenbacher's Gourmet Butter Microwave Popping Corn; unpopped kernels discarded and finely crushed*
¼ cup all-purpose flour
2 tsps seasoned salt
1½ tsps curry powder
1 tsp paprika
¼ tsp *each*: garlic powder and black pepper
⅛ tsp ground cloves
6 loin-end pork chops
1 egg lightly beaten with 1 Tbsp water

Sauce
1 Tbsp butter or margarine
1 cup orange juice
6 Tbsps corn syrup
1½ Tbsps cornstarch
Pinch salt
1½ Tbsps Grand Marnier Liqueur
1 (11oz) can mandarin oranges, drained

1. Preheat oven to 350°F. Have ready a foil-lined baking sheet sprayed with cooking spray.

2. In medium size bowl, combine *first 8* ingredients; set aside.

3. In small bowl, dip *each* pork chop in egg wash, then into popcorn mixture, coating well.

4. Place pork chops on baking sheet. Bake for 40 minutes or until done, turning chops over half-way through baking.

STEP 4

5. Five minutes before serving, melt butter in a small saucepan; stir in orange juice, corn syrup, cornstarch and salt. Continue to cook over low heat, stirring constantly until thickened.

6. Add liqueur and oranges, cooking only until heated through. Serve over pork chops.

STEP 6

Cook's Notes

TIME: Preparation takes 20 minutes, baking takes 40 minutes.

PREPARATION:* To finely crush popcorn, use a blender or food processor.

COOK'S TIPS: Coatin' Note. Place flour, popcorn and spices in a gallon-size plastic zip bag. It'll coat chops beautifully without any mess.

DOWN HOME INSIDE-OUT TURKEY PIE

Serves 4 to 6

This hearty entree will warm you up-from the inside-out and we're sure it'll be gobbled up in a jiffy.

Wesson No-Stick Cooking Spray
1 cup water
¾ cup diced celery
2 Tbsps butter
1 bag popped Orville Redenbacher's Gourmet
    Light Butter Microwave Popping Corn,
    unpopped kernels discarded
½ tsp sage
¼ tsp pepper
⅛ tsp garlic powder
2 (2.8oz) cans French fried onions
1 egg, lightly beaten
2 cups cooked cubed turkey
1 (10¾oz) can condensed cream of chicken soup
1 (10oz) bag frozen peas and carrots, thawed and
    well drained

1. Preheat oven to 350°F. Spray a 9-inch souffle dish with cooking spray.

2. In saucepan, simmer water, celery and butter for seven minutes.

3. Meanwhile, in a large bowl, combine popped corn, sage, pepper and garlic powder.

4. Pour celery broth over popcorn mixture; stir. Add *1 can* onions and egg to popcorn mixture; blend well.

5. Spoon stuffing into soufflé dish, pressing the stuffing evenly on the bottom and up the sides.

STEP 5

6. In a medium bowl, combine cooked turkey, soup, peas and carrots.

7. Pour ½ the filling into the stuffing crust then add ½ *can* onions; repeat with *remaining* filling and onions. When sprinkling onions on top of filling, leave a 1½-inch border.

STEP 7

8. Cover and bake for 35 to 40 minutes or until heated through.

Cook's Notes

⏱ TIME: Preparation takes 15 minutes, baking takes 40 minutes.

🍞 COOK'S TIP: Gobbled-D-Good! You may substitute 2 cups cubed cooked chicken for the turkey. This is a great leftovers recipe!

GIDEE-UP LIL' CORN DOGGIES

Makes 20 Mini Corn Dogs

Mini in size, but full of that special flavor. The secret is in the freshly-ground popcorn!

---

5 cups Wesson Oil
2 cups popped Orville Redenbacher's Gourmet Original Popping Corn, unpopped kernels discarded and finely crushed*
1 cup all-purpose flour
3 Tbsps sugar
1½ tsps baking powder
½ tsp salt
2 Tbsps vegetable shortening
1 egg
1 cup milk
1 lb (5-inch) frankfurters, cut into halves crosswise
20 (6-inch) wooden skewers

---

1. Heat oil in 2-quart saucepan to 350°F.

2. In medium bowl, combine crushed popped corn, flour, sugar, baking powder and salt.

3. Cut in shortening until mixture is crumbly; add

STEP 3

egg and milk. Beat vigorously, by hand, until mixture is smooth.

STEP 5

4. Insert wooden skewer into round end of *each* frank half. Dip *each* frank in batter; hold upside down by skewer and allow excess batter to run off. Franks should be evenly coated.

STEP 4

5. Place coated franks into oil allowing oil to completely cover. Fry until brown on all sides, turning franks with long-handled tongs.

6. Drain on paper towels and serve immediately.

Cook's Notes

⏱ TIME: Preparation and cooking takes 35 minutes.

◤ PREPARATION:* To finely crush popcorn, use a blender or food processor.

📖 COOK'S TIP: Freezing Fido? Make a double batch of corn dogs as they freeze well! Simply individually wrap cooled, cooked corn dogs in plastic wrap, then wrap tightly in foil. Let thaw and reheat in 375°F oven until heated through.

INDIANA COUNTRY FRIED CHICKEN

Serves 6

If it's possible to beat the taste of mother's fried chicken, this may be the way!

Wesson Oil
3 lbs frying chicken pieces
2 quarts popped Orville Redenbacher's Gourmet
    Butter Microwave Popping Corn, unpopped
    kernels discarded and finely crushed*
½ cup all-purpose flour
½ tsp *each*: pepper and seasoned salt
2 eggs, lightly beaten with 1 Tablespoon water

---

1. Fill a large, heavy skillet to ½ its depth with oil. Preheat oil to 325°F.

STEP 1

2. Wash chicken and pat dry.

3. Combine crushed popped corn, flour, pepper and salt in a bag; close bag and shake vigorously to blend ingredients.

STEP 4

4. Dip a few pieces of chicken in egg mixture, then shake chicken in flour mixture until generously coated. If necessary, press on coating with fingertips to completely coat.

5. Fry chicken, starting skin side up, 20 to 30 minutes or until cooked through. Turn once halfway through cooking.

STEP 5

Cook's Notes

⏱ TIME: Preparation takes 15 minutes, frying takes 40 to 60 minutes.

◆ PREPARATION:* To finely crush popcorn, use a blender or food processor.

❓ VARIATION: Tender Moments. To prepare chicken tenders as an appetizer, use the above recipe substituting 2-inch long strips of boneless chicken. Fry until golden and serve with dipping sauce. Remember this idea for your next picnic!

DOUBLE-YOUR-FUN FRUIT PIZZA

Makes 12 wedges

Two of the great pleasures of life are popcorn and pizza! Here, we've combined popped corn, and fruit-a-plenty in this beautiful and easy pizza-style pie!

1 quart popped Orville Redenbacher's Gourmet
   Popping Corn, unpopped kernels discarded
   and finely crushed*
2 cups all-purpose flour
1 cup butter, softened
¾ cup powdered sugar
2 Tbsps lemon juice
2 tsps lemon peel
1 (8oz) pkg. cream cheese, softened
½ cup *each*: sugar and sour cream
1 tsp vanilla extract
**6 cups assorted fruit, fresh, frozen or canned,
   well-drained (suggested fruits: berries, kiwi,
   pineapple, halved red or green grapes,
   bananas, peaches and/or nectarines, and
   apples).

1. Preheat oven to 350°F. Have ready a well greased 12-inch pizza pan.

2. In small bowl, combine ground corn and flour; set aside.

3. In medium bowl, cream butter and sugar. Add lemon juice, lemon peel and corn mixture, mixing until well-blended.

4. Press mixture into pizza pan; bake for 20 to 25 minutes or until golden brown. Let cool 30 minutes.

5. Meanwhile, in small bowl, beat cream cheese, sugar, sour cream and vanilla with electric mixer until smooth. Refrigerate until needed.

6. Spread cheese mixture over cooled crust.

STEP 7

7. Beginning in the center of the pizza, arrange fruit in circles. Arrange smaller amounts of fruit in the center and the larger amounts of fruit around the edges.

8. Refrigerate at least 30 minutes before serving; cut into wedges.

Cook's Notes

🕐 TIME: Preparation takes 25 minutes, baking takes is 30 minutes and chilling takes 30 minutes.

🍴 COOK'S TIP: In-a-Crunch? If you're short on time, prepare the crust and cream cheese filling the day before. Crust may be stored, well covered, at room temperature. Refrigerate the filling until ready to use.

🔪 PREPARATION: *To finely crush popcorn, use a blender or food processor.** Peel, if necessary, and thinly slice fruit. If using bananas, peaches, nectarines or apples, protect from darkening by slicing into a mixture of 1 teaspoon lemon juice and 1 quart water.

OUT-OF-THIS-WORLD CHOCOLATE TOFFEE CAKE

Makes one 9-inch Double Layer Cake

No where on earth can you get closer to heaven than with this cake!

1 (1 lb 2.25oz) box yellow cake mix
Wesson No-Stick Cooking Spray
2 lbs prepared fudge-flavored frosting
1 bag popped Orville Redenbacher's Gourmet
   Butter Toffee Microwave Popping Corn,
   unpopped kernels discarded and *lightly*
   crushed
4 (1.4oz) bars milk chocolate-coated English toffee,
   crushed
1½ cups coarsely crushed unsalted roasted peanuts
½ cup fudge topping, warmed

1. Prepare cake mix according to package instructions to make two 9-inch round cakes; cool.

2. Place *1 round* layer on cake plate. Generously frost the top of the cake with frosting.

STEP 2

3. In large bowl, combine popcorn, toffee candy and nuts; mix well. Slowly drizzle fudge topping over popcorn mixture while stirring.

STEP 4

4. Sprinkle and lightly press with fingertips 1½ cups popcorn mixture onto frosting, leaving a 1-inch border.

5. Place *second round* layer over the first. Frost the entire cake with the *remaining* frosting.

STEP 6

6. Using your hand, *lightly* press the *remaining* popcorn mixture onto the frosting; cover the entire cake.

7. Serve with vanilla ice cream or whipped cream.

Cook's Notes

🕐 TIME: Preparation and baking takes 50 minutes.

📖 COOK'S TIP: Show Off! This delicious cake will make family and friends "oh" and "ah". To cut it with ease, use a serrated knife and a pie server.

CARAMEL CRUNCH CHEESECAKE

Makes one 10-inch cheesecake

It's hard to describe the balance between the smooth, creamy filling and the caramel crust. You'll just have to experience it!

Crust
1 bag popped Orville Redenbacher's Gourmet Caramel Microwave Popping Corn, unpopped kernels discarded
¾ cup sugar
½ cup all-purpose flour
⅓ cup butter or margarine, melted
1 tsp cinnamon

Filling
2 (8oz) pkgs. cream cheese
1 cup sugar
3 eggs
2 tsps vanilla extract
¾ tsp almond extract
3 cups sour cream

STEP 4

6. Meanwhile, in a large bowl, using an electric mixer on low speed, mix *all* filling ingredients *except* sour cream until smooth.

STEP 7

1. Preheat oven to 350°F. Have ready a 10-inch spring-form pan.

2. Reserve *1½ cups* popped popcorn for topping; set aside. Using a food processor, finely crush *remaining* popcorn.

3. In a medium bowl, combine crushed popcorn and *remaining* crust ingredients; mix until moistened.

4. Place crust mixture in spring-form pan. Firmly press the crust mixture on the bottom and 1-inch up the sides of the pan.

5. Bake for 10 minutes; cool.

7. Fold in the sour cream until blended; pour filling into crust.

8. Bake 60 to 70 minutes.

9. *Turn oven off* and allow cake to completely cool in oven with door slightly open (about 1½ hours).

10. Lightly crush *remaining* popcorn; sprinkle over the top of the cheesecake. Refrigerate overnight.

Cook's Notes

TIME: Preparation takes 20 minutes, baking takes 70 minutes and oven cooling takes 1½ hours. Refrigerate overnight.

COOK'S TIP: Hold It! Discarding unpopped kernels is a fact-of-popcorn-life! Before you prepare a recipe, it is a *must* to sift through popped corn and discard those kernels remaining unpopped!

GOOD MORNING CHEERY CHERRY COFFEE CAKE

Serves 8

Forget snap & crackle! Go for pop, pop, pop, and the fragrant aroma of hot, fruity, fresh coffee cake. It is going to be a great day!

Streusel
¼ cup sugar
3 Tbsps butter or margarine, softened
½ tsp cinnamon
3 cup popped Orville Redenbacher's Gourmet Original Popping Corn, unpopped kernels discarded and lightly crushed
½ cup all-purpose flour
¼ cup chopped nuts

Cake
2 cups all-purpose baking mix
⅔ cup milk
¼ cup sugar
2 Tbsps Wesson Oil
1 egg
½ (21oz) can cherry pie filling or favorite pie filling

Icing
1 cup powdered sugar
1 Tbsp water
1 tsp vanilla

---

1. Preheat oven to 350°F. Have ready a greased 9-inch pie dish.

2. In a bowl, cream together sugar and butter; stir in cinnamon. Add *remaining* streusel ingredients; blend until crumbly; set aside.

3. In a medium mixing bowl, combine *all* the cake ingredients together *except* pie filling; mix well.

4. Pour cake mixture into pie dish.

STEP 5

5. Sprinkle ½ streusel over cake. Pour pie filling evenly over streusel; sprinkle with *remaining* streusel.

6. Bake for 40 to 45 minutes or until wooden pick in center comes out clean; cool for 15 minutes.

7. Meanwhile, in a small bowl, combine *all* icing ingredients; mix until smooth. Drizzle icing over coffee cake.

STEP 7

Cook's Notes

⌚ TIME: Preparation takes 15 minutes. baking takes 45 minutes.

? VARIATION: To tell the Truth! We cannot tell a lie. Cherries are not the only filling you can use to make this sumptuous coffee cake. Try apple, blueberry or any pie filling that tickles your taste buds.

PATCH QUILT VALENTINE HEART

Serves 6 to 8

Share this Valentine with those you love.

Wesson No-Stick Cooking Spray
½ cup *each*: corn syrup and cinnamon red hot candies
½ tsp salt
2 quarts popped Orville Redenbacher's Gourmet Original Popping Corn, unsalted, unpopped kernels discarded
1 (4.25oz) tube *each*: red and white decorating icing
Vanilla ice cream
Peppermints, maraschino cherries, red hots and silver dragees

STEP 5

6. Scoop ice cream into popcorn heart and evenly spread until ice cream has filled the entire popcorn cavity and it is one level.

7. Pipe icing onto ice cream to form a patch quilt pattern.

1. Have ready a 9-inch heart-shaped pan sprayed with cooking spray.

2. In 3-quart saucepan, on medium-low heat, stir together corn syrup, cinnamon candy and salt until candy dissolves.

3. Add popcorn, stirring gently, until completely coated. Reserve ⅛ *cup* mixture; set aside.

4. Pour popcorn mixture in pan, pressing firmly together on bottom and sides of pan.

5. With fingertips, gently pull down the popcorn at top of the "V" in the heart to give the shape a more prominent heart shape effect; let cool. Remove from pan; place on serving plate.

STEP 7

8. Fill *each* square with candies and *remaining* popcorn.

9. Freeze at least 1 hour before serving.

Cook's Notes

🕐 TIME: Preparation takes 40 minutes, freezing takes 1 hour.

📖 COOK'S TIP: Darn It! You don't have a heart shaped pan? Use an 8-inch round pan instead – it'll still be made with love!

CHOCOLATE SNACKIN' JACKS

Serves 8

Reminiscent of the sweet treats we all loved, this snack is a hit with any age group.

2½ qts. popped Orville Redenbacher's Gourmet Original Popping Corn, unpopped kernels discarded
¾ cup *each*: sugar and firmly-packed light brown sugar
⅓ cup light corn syrup
3 Tbsps butter or margarine
1½ Tbsps water
½ tsp cream of tartar
½ cup unsweetened cocoa powder, sifted
1 tsp baking soda
1 cup *each*: pecan halves and shredded sweetened coconut
8 small zip-top bags
8 assorted small party trinkets (i.e. whistles, rings, etc.)

---

1. Have ready 2 greased long-handled wooden spoons and a large sheet of greased wax paper.

2. Place popped corn in large bowl; set aside.

STEP 3

3. In 2-quart saucepan, heat *next 6 ingredients* to 280°F on candy thermometer; remove from heat.

4. Immediately stir in cocoa powder and baking soda; add pecans and coconut.

STEP 5

5. Working quickly, pour mixture over popped corn, using wooden spoons; toss to evenly coat corn mixture.

6. Spread mixture onto wax paper; cool 15 minutes.

STEP 6

7. Divide cooled mixture evenly into *8 portions* and place in bags with 1 trinket per bag. Seal *each* bag air-tight.

Cook's Notes

: Preparation and cooling takes 35

🍳 COOK'S TIP: Pot Shot. Use a heavy, deep, straight-sided pot to reduce risk of boiling syrup burning. Long-handled wooden spoons and a candy thermometer are the best tools of the confection-making trade!

AN APPLE-A-DAY CARAMEL APPLES

Makes 6 apples

Keep plenty of these apples around, as they'll go faster than you can dip 'em!

1 (14oz) pkg. caramels, unwrapped
2 Tbsps water
6 wooden sticks
6 small Granny Smith apples, washed, dried and
    stems removed
1 bag popped Orville Redenbacher's Gourmet
    Caramel Microwave Popping Corn, unpopped
    kernels discarded and lightly crushed

STEP 2

2. Insert wooden sticks into stem end of *each* apple. Dip apples, one at a time, into hot* caramel sauce; turn until coated. Allow excess to drip off apples.

1. In 1½ quart saucepan, melt caramels and water over low heat, stirring occasionally, until melted and smooth. Remove from heat.

STEP 3

3. Immediately press popped corn onto apple. Set on wax paper; store in refrigerator.

4. Before serving, let stand at room temperature 15 minutes to allow caramel to soften.

STEP 1

Cook's Notes

🕐 TIME: Preparation takes 30 minutes.

📖 COOK'S TIP:* If caramel sauce hardens too quickly, return to low heat until softened.

❓ VARIATION: Switch Hit. Switch Orville's Caramel Corn with his Toffee Corn in this recipe. It's sure to be a hit.

MOON ROCKS

Makes 1½ dozen cookies

You don't need to be an astronaut to have a collection of these out-of-this-world cookies on your counter!

3 egg whites, at room temperature
¼ tsp cream of tartar
¾ cup sugar
1 tsp vanilla extract
5 cups popped Orville Redenbacher's Gourmet Original Popping Corn, unpopped kernels discarded
1 (8oz) pkg. colorful candy-coated chocolate pieces

1. Preheat oven to 275°F. Have ready 2 greased, wax paper-lined baking sheets.

2. In medium bowl, beat egg whites and cream of tartar on high speed with electric mixer until soft peaks form.

STEP 2

3. Add sugar, *2 Tablespoons* at a time, and

continue beating until stiff peaks form. Beat in vanilla.

STEP 4

4. Gently fold in popped corn and chocolate pieces.

5. Drop heaping *Tablespoons* of mixture onto baking sheets.

STEP 5

6. Bake *each* sheet *separately* for 50 to 60 minutes or until light golden brown. Let cool 30 minutes.

7. Remove from baking sheets and store in airtight container.

Cook's Notes

⏱ TIME: Preparation takes 15 minutes, baking takes 60 minutes.

🍳 COOK'S TIP: Rocks from Mars. Use a double-dose of green food coloring (or any color) for a treat your little martians can eat.

SPARKLIN' PEANUT BUTTER POPCORN BALLS

Makes 8 Popcorn Balls

Colorful and quick, kids of all ages will enjoy these chewy treats.

Assorted candy/sugar sprinkles
4 cups miniature marshmallows
¼ cup butter or margarine
⅓ cup Peter Pan Peanut Butter
7½ cups popped Orville Redenbacher's Gourmet Original Popping Corn, unpopped kernels discarded

STEP 4

1. Place sprinkles in individual small bowls; set aside.

2. In a 4-quart saucepan, melt marshmallows and butter over low heat, stirring constantly until smooth.

4. Add popped corn to peanut butter mixture; stir until well coated.

5. With buttered fingers, quickly shape popcorn into eight *2½-inch balls*; then roll balls firmly in sprinkles to coat well.

STEP 2

3. Remove from heat; stir in peanut butter until mixture is smooth.

STEP 5

Cook's Notes

⏱ TIME: Preparation takes 30 minutes.

🎩 COOK'S TIP: Sticky Situation? To smoothly form popcorn balls, lightly butter your hands and we do hope they're sparkling clean!

MONKEY BUSINESS FROZEN BANANAS

Makes 6 Frozen Bananas

Hey! Who covered my banana with deep dark chocolate and rolled it in crushed popcorn?! Well . . . THANKS!

6 small bananas, peeled and refrigerated
1 bag popped Orville Redenbacher's Gourmet
    Butter Toffee Microwave Popping Corn,
    unpopped kernels discarded and lightly
    crushed
1 (12oz) bag chocolate morsels
2 Tbsps shortening
6 wooden skewers or popsicle sticks

1. Have ready a wax paper-lined baking sheet.

2. Pour crushed popcorn in medium bowl; set aside.

3. Melt together chocolate and shortening, blend well. Place melted chocolate in an 8 x 8 x 2-inch baking dish.

STEP 4

4. Quickly roll banana in chocolate sauce or brush it on.

5. Then quickly roll coated banana in crushed popcorn; coat evenly. Place on baking sheet.

STEP 5

6. Repeat steps 4 and 5 with *remaining* bananas.

7. Freeze bananas for 20 minutes or eat immediately after coating.

STEP 3

Cook's Notes

TIME: Preparation takes 25 minutes.

? VARIATION: Over The Rainbow. Pastel meltaway candies, which are available at craft or party stores, make wonderful coatings for bananas. Simply melt them according to package directions and follow the same directions above.

POP-O-LANTERN

Makes 1 Pumpkin

This be-'witch'-ing pumpkin won't scare anyone, but, instead, will be a real treat!

---

4 quarts popped Orville Redenbacher's Gourmet Original Popping Corn, unpopped kernels discarded
1 cup *each*: sugar and corn syrup
½ tsp salt
Orange food color
Black licorice vines
2 licorice buttons
1 (4.25oz) tube orange decorating icing, optional
Wooden picks
2 candy orange slices
1 small yellow gum drop
Candy corn
3 to 4 large green gum drops, rolled out and trimmed
1 black witch's hat, optional

---

1. In large bowl, place popcorn; set aside.

2. In small saucepan, over medium heat, combine sugar, corn syrup, salt and food color, stirring constantly, until mixture comes to a boil and sugar dissolves.

3. Pour over popcorn; stir until well coated.

4. With greased hands*, press popcorn firmly together into pumpkin shape. Set aside to cool and harden slightly.

5. Cut licorice vines to proper lengths. Press licorice from bottom center to top center of pumpkin, tucking licorice ends into the top center.

STEP 5

6. For eyes, press licorice buttons into pumpkin (secure with decorating icing, if desired).

7. Using wooden picks, insert candy orange slices for ears and yellow gum drop for nose.

8. Arrange candy corn for teeth and 3 green gum drops for leaves.

9. Place witch's hat on top, OR use a large, green gum drop to make a stem.

STEP 3

Cook's Notes

⏱ TIME: Preparation takes 20 minutes, decorating takes 15 minutes.

🍳 COOK'S TIP: * Use caution when handling sugar mixture; it may be hot.

❓ VARIATION: Gobs-o-Goblins! Instead of making one big pumpkin, shape the popcorn mixture to make several mini-pumpkins. You can even change the food coloring and candies to create ghosts, black cats, witches or other spooks.

NINA'S EVER-GREEN CHRISTMAS TREE

Makes 1 Tree

"O, Christmas Tree! O, Christmas Tree!" how lovely my holiday table will look with you on center stage!

Wesson No-Stick Cooking Spray
8 quarts popped Orville Redenbacher's Gourmet Original Popping Corn, unpopped kernels discarded
2 cups *each*: sugar and corn syrup
1 tsp salt
Green food color
Assorted gum balls and/or small jaw breakers
1 (4.25oz) tube white decorating icing
1 (0.5oz) pkg. Chiclets brand, tiny-size, flavor-coated gum
1 (12 piece) box Chiclets brand, fruit-flavor gum silver dragees
1 star (purchase at craft store)

1. Have ready a baking sheet sprayed with cooking spray; set aside.

2. In two large bowls, divide popcorn; set aside.

3. In saucepan, over medium heat, combine sugar, corn syrup, salt and food color, stirring constantly, until mixture comes to a boil and sugar dissolves. Immediately pour over popcorn, dividing equally.

4. Working quickly, toss popcorn until well coated; pour onto baking sheet.

5. With greased* hands, press popcorn firmly

together into a tree shape (approximately 10-inch high).

STEP 5

6. Once desired shape is achieved, press gum balls, jaw breakers and gum into tree. (If necessary, you may use icing to hold candy in place.)

7. Squeeze icing onto tree simulating snow.

8. Press silver dragees into "snow" and place star on top of tree.

STEP 7

Cook's Notes

⏱ TIME: Preparation takes 20 minutes, decorating takes 25 minutes.

🍳 COOK'S TIP:* Use caution when handling sugar mixture; it may be hot.

❓ VARIATION: White Christmas. For a white-flocked tree, simply eliminate green food color and use lots and lots of white decorating icing.

MR. AND MRS. BUNNY-POP

Makes 2 Bunnies

Hop into spring with this adorable, edible centerpiece that you can create with your children.

6 quarts popped Orville Redenbacher's Gourmet
    Original Popping Corn, unpopped kernels
    discarded
1 cup *each*: sugar and corn syrup
½ tsp salt
12 plain, round, wooden picks
6 raisins
2 pink candies
2 *each*: pink and blue pipe cleaners
1 *each*: black hat and 5-inch white doily or bonnet
Bow tie, made from black construction paper
Pastel plaid ribbon, ¼-inch wide
1 small plastic basket, filled with fruit-flavored
    decors, optional
Pink Easter grass (optional)

STEP 3

STEP 4

1. In large bowl, place popcorn; set aside.

2. In saucepan, combine sugar, corn syrup and salt, stirring constantly, until mixture comes to a boil and sugar dissolves; pour over popcorn. Stir until well coated.

3. Working quickly, with greased hands*, press popcorn firmly together, making *2 large* balls for bodies, *2 medium* balls for heads, and *2 small* balls for tails.

4. Press heads and tails onto bodies. (May use wooden picks to hold together, if necessary.) Allow to cool and harden before decorating.

5. Insert *3 wooden* picks on *each* side of bunnys' faces for whiskers.

6. Press raisins into popcorn for eyes and noses. (May use wooden picks, if necessary.)

7. Press pink candies into popcorn for mouths.

8. Insert pipe cleaners through hat or doily into "heads" for ears.

9. Make bow tie for Mr. Bunny-Pop and press into place.

10. Tie ribbon around Mrs. Bunny-Pop's neck.

11. Arrange candy-filled basket and grass at the base of bunnies, if desired.

Cook's Notes

⌐ TIME: Preparation takes ½ hour, decorating takes ½ hour.

♟ COOK'S TIP:* Use caution when handling sugar mixture; it may be hot.

❓ VARIATION: For Pete's Sake (Peter Rabbit, that is!) Arrange fresh tulips, lillies or other spring flowers with these adorable bunnies to create a centerpiece that says, "Celebrate"!

CREEPY CRAWLY CREATURES

Whimsical and what fun! Celebrate spring with these edible garden-like creatures.

½ cup butter or margarine
1 (10½oz) bag miniature marshmallows (6 cups)
10 drops green food color
⅛ tsp mint flavoring
4 quarts popped Orville Redenbacher's Gourmet Popping Corn, discard unpopped kernels and unsalted
16 chocolate sandwich cookies
1 pkg. black licorice vines, cut into 80 2-inch lengths
1 pkg. assorted small gum drops

---

1. In 5-quart Dutch oven, melt butter; stir in marshmallows, food color and flavoring and cook over low heat until melted and well-blended.

2. Turn off heat; stir in popcorn until well-coated.

3. With greased hands*, using ½ cup measure, form into 16 balls.

4. Place *each* ball on top of a cookie. Divide ball/base into 4 groups of 4 to form *4 creatures.*

STEP 4

STEP 5

5. Gently push *2 pieces* of licorice into the "heads" of *each* creature for their antennas.

6. Press 6 *"legs"* (3 on each side) of licorice between *each* popcorn ball and cookie; repeat with *remaining* balls and cookies.

STEP 6

7. Press *2 to 3* gum drops into the top of *each* ball for "spine".

8. Cut gum drops in half for eyes and mouth; press cut-side into ball to make the "face".

Cook's Notes

⏱ TIME: Preparation takes 20 minutes, decorating takes 30 minutes.

👨‍🍳 COOK'S TIP:* Use caution when handling popcorn mixture; it may be hot.

❓ VARIATION: Bug Me! By changing food coloring and flavors, create a garden full of lady bugs, honey bees or what ever your imagination will run "wild" with!

INDEX

Photography by Peter Barry
Recipes prepared and styled by Helen Burdett
Designed by Judith Chant
Edited by Jillian Stewart
Project co-ordination by Hanni Penrose